The Kids'
Library of
Personal Safety™

A Kid's Guide
to Staying Safe on the

STREETS

Maribeth Boelts

The Rosen Publishing Group's
PowerKids Press™
New York

Published in 1997 by The Rosen Publishing Group, Inc.
29 East 21st Street, New York, NY 10010

First Edition

Book Design: Erin McKenna

Photo Illustrations and Credits: pp. 4, 15, 19 by Seth Dinnerman; pp. 7, 20 © Ron Chapple/FPG International Corp.; p. 8 © Mark Kozlowski/FPG International Corp.; p. 11 © P. Degginger/H. Armstrong Roberts, Inc.; p. 12 © Jacob Toposchaner/FPG International Corp.; p. 16 by Katherine Hsu.

Boelts, Maribeth, 1964–
    A kid's guide to staying safe on the streets / by Maribeth Boelts.
        p.   cm. — (The kids' library of personal safety)
    Includes index.
    Summary: Discusses ways children can be safe around strangers, traffic, and other potentially dangerous situations.
  ISBN 0-8239-5080-8
  1. Safety Education—Juvenile literature. 2. Traffic safety and children—Juvenile literature.
  3. Accidents—Prevention—Juvenile literature. 4. Children and strangers—Juvenile literature.
  5. Children—Crimes against—Prevention—Juvenile films. [1. Safety.] I. Title. II. Series.
HV675.5.B636 1997
613.6—dc21   96-54271
                                                       CIP
                                                       AC

Manufactured in the United States of America

Contents

Smart, Safe Choices

As you get older, you will be able to do more things on your own. You may be allowed to walk home after school with your friends. You may go to the park or the playground by yourself. You may cross streets by yourself or ride your bike around the neighborhood.

All of these things show that you are growing up. But doing these things on your own also means being able to make smart and safe choices.

A part of growing up is learning to do some things on your own.

Jill

    As Jill left the library, a car pulled up. "Would you like a ride?" the driver asked. Jill did not know the driver of the car. Her parents had told her never to ride with someone she didn't know. Jill walked away from the car and back into the library. Jill called her parents for a ride instead. The man in the car looked nice, but Jill made the safe choice by calling home. She knew never to accept a ride from a **stranger** (STRAYN-jer).

Be smart: Memorize your phone number so you can call home if you need to. ▶

Strangers

A stranger is a person you don't know. Many strangers are nice people. But some strangers could try to hurt you. There are things you can do to keep yourself safe from strangers.

- Never talk to strangers.
- Do not take money, gifts, or rides from strangers.
- Never accept food or candy from strangers.

If a stranger comes over to you, walk or run away quickly. Tell a grown-up you trust that a stranger came up to you.

Never get into a car with someone you don't know.

9

It's a Secret

Having a **secret code word** (SEE-krit KOHD WERD) with your family will help to keep you safe. If there is an **emergency** (ee-MER-jen-see) and someone you don't know has to take you somewhere, your parents will tell the person the word. When that person says the secret code word to you, you will know it's okay to go with him or her. If he or she doesn't know the secret word, don't go with that person.

10

You and your parent can decide together on a code word that you will both remember. ▶

Safe Routes

Your parents can help you choose the best **routes** (ROWTS) to take to school or to a friend's house. If you live close to the library or to stores, your parents can help you choose routes to take to those places too. Once you decide on a route, you can practice walking that route with your parents. Then you can walk it on your own. Your mom or dad can show you where to cross streets and where you can go for help if you have trouble.

◀ You can show your safe route to a friend, and both of you can walk together.

13

Traffic Safety

No matter where you're going, it is always best to go with friends. Use the sidewalk when you walk somewhere. If there is no sidewalk, walk on the left side of the road, facing traffic. When you're ready to cross, go to a corner if you can. This is what you do next:

1. Stop at the curb or edge of the road. Never run out into the street.
2. Listen and look for traffic to the left, to the right, and then to the left again.
3. Wait until the street is clear. Stay **alert** (uh-LERT) as you cross the street.

You can never be too careful ▶ when crossing the street.

Dangerous Places

Some places are never safe for kids to play in. Stay away from empty buildings, alleys, **construction** (kun-STRUKT-shun) areas, and other places that your parents have told you are unsafe. Don't go to playgrounds that have broken equipment or lots of garbage. Watch for signs that say, "KEEP OUT" or "DANGER." The signs are there to keep people from getting hurt.

◀ Empty areas, such as this parking lot, may look like fun places to play but they can be dangerous if there is litter or broken glass.

17

"What If?"

A game called "What If?" can help you find out more about being safe in your **neighborhood** (NAY-ber-hood). In the game, your parents or another adult that you trust asks you questions such as "What if you were walking to school and a man asked you to help him find his lost puppy?" or "What if your friend wanted you to take a shortcut to her house?" or "What if you saw someone throw a rock at a store window?"

You can answer the questions using what you know about safety.

18

As you answer the questions in the "What If" game, you'll be learning how to stay safe. ▶

911

There are times when you may need emergency help. If you are hurt, if someone is in trouble, or if you need to report a fire, call 911. All you have to do is pick up the phone and dial 911.

An **operator** (OP-er-ay-ter) will answer. Tell the operator you need help. Stay calm and listen to what he tells you. The operator will ask for your name, where you are calling from, and what the emergency is. Don't hang up until he tells you to. The operator will then call an ambulance or the fire department and send them to help you.

◀ Staying calm and calling 911 is important.

21

Staying Safe and Alert

You can help keep your neighborhood safe by staying alert. Being alert means paying attention to what is going on around you. If you're on your way to school and notice something strange in your neighborhood, such as a broken door on your neighbor's house or smoke coming from an apartment window, tell a grown-up or call 911 right away.

Staying smart and alert helps keep you, your family, and your friends safe.

Glossary

alert (uh-LERT) Being careful and paying attention.

construction (kun-STRUKT-shun) Building or putting something together.

emergency (ee-MER-jen-see) A sudden need for quick action.

neighborhood (NAY-ber-hood) An area in which people live.

operator (OP-er-ay-ter) A person who is ready to help you or give you information on the telephone.

route (ROWT) The path you take to get somewhere.

secret code word (SEE-krit KOHD WERD) A word that only you and your parents know.

stranger (STRAYN-jer) Someone that you or your family does not know.

Index

A
alert, being, 14, 22

C
choices, making, 5, 6
construction, 17

E
emergency, 10, 21

F
friends, 5, 14, 18, 22

G
going places alone, 5, 13
growing up, 5
grown-ups, 9, 22

N
neighborhood, 18, 22
911, calling, 21, 22

O
operator, 21

P
parents, 6, 13, 17, 18

R
routes, safe, 13

S
secret code word, 10
strangers, 6, 9

T
traffic rules, 14

W
"What If?" game, 18

24